C01

Brentwood
in old picture postcards

Frank D. Simpson

European Library   *ZALTBOMMEL/THE NETHERLANDS*

Cover picture:
Upper High Street Brentwood in 1843 as depicted in a charming water colour painting by J.P. Andre, viewed from a point opposite the present Post Office. The date is just a year or two after the opening of the Eastern Counties Railway, the resulting quietude as the traffic was taken off the road seems to be reflected here. The third property on the left is the Chequers Inn close by the old chapel, it now became little more than a local public house. See plate 9.

GB ISBN 90 288 4794 4

© 1989 European Library – Zaltbommel/The Netherlands

Second edition, 2001: reprint of the original edition of 1989.

European Library
post office box 49
NL – 5300 AA Zaltbommel/The Netherlands
telephone: 0031 418 513144
fax: 0031 418 515515
e-mail:publisher@eurobib.nl

INTRODUCTION

I am pleased to say that the book 'Brentwood in old picture postcards' evoked sufficient interest to require a second and third edition, and also some enquiries asking if a further selection of old pictures of the town and neighbourhood could be published. Although the book gave fairly wide coverage of the district, examination of my collection showed there were still sufficient hitherto unpublished photographs, postcards and other material to fill another small volume which I felt should be made available for the enjoyment of all who are interested in the town and the way it used to look.

Much contained within the introduction to the original volume holds good here and need not be repeated. However, the use of some earlier material does call for a few additional remarks. The coming of the railway shown within did have a profound effect on the town, its convenient distance from London and its exceptionally pleasant location produced an immediate demand for residences by 'city gentlemen', and new housing soon sprang up. Its other effect was to draw off all but the local traffic from the Great Road to all parts of East Anglia which passed through. Fortunately the new development on the town largely mitigated the above effects which caused a serious decline in some towns dependent on the road traffic.

During preparations for the railway, the directors took a survey of the road traffic on this road in order to estimate the traffic potential. This was taken over several weeks at the Whalebone Gate (Chadwell Heath) and at Widford (near Chelmsford) from which the following daily numbers have been extracted, after deducting traffic which either turned off or did not proceed beyond Romford. There were 41 coaches proceeding beyond Brentwood and a further 12 which stopped or turned off to Southend, Billericay, Ongar or Herongate. Two worked from the town by Mr. Murrell, who had a coach office near the cross roads, anticipating the travel agent as he booked passengers for all coaches passing through.

Private carriages, gigs and the like totalled 85, also 4 fish vans came through from Leigh or Maldon, and 11 stage waggons and 14 taxed carts passed. Livestock travelling on the hoof reached the large daily total of 265 bulls, 522 sheep, 35 calves and 48 pigs, almost all destined for the London markets. At Christmas time large numbers of turkeys and geese could be seen, some driven all the way from Norfolk.

The original civil parish of Brentwood was formed towards the end of the last century from quite a small portion of the large and ancient parish of South Weald; it comprised only 460 acres whereas the latter still contained 4,654 acres. At first it was designated the Brentwood Urban Sanitary Authority, but in 1897 elevated to the status of Urban District Council.

Why its boundaries were so drawn is now difficult of comprehension for at the time of formation the town was already spilling over into those parts of Shenfield, Great Warley or South Weald contiguous with the town. As these parishes were administered by the Billericay or Romford Rural District Councils some anomolous situations arose in connection with such matters as sewage disposal, burial of the dead, fire fighting and so on which required the setting up of joint committees.

A sketch map showing the disposition of the former parish boundaries follows this introduction. Among the peculiarities of this arrangement is the fact that the whole of Brentwood railway station lies within Shenfield parish, and that the west side of Warley Hill was administered from Billericay and the east side came partly under Billericay and partly under Romford! There was a point in the centre of the road near the Essex Arms public house where one could be standing in all three administrative areas at the same time.

Fortuitously, any complications arising in local government

were to some extent simplified by one man: he was the redoubtable C. Edgar Lewis, a local solicitor with a thriving practice who was already holding the office of Coroner for South Essex, who now became Clerk to both the Brentwood U.D.C. and the Billericay R.D.C., and of the dependent joint committees. It will be seen that Lewis will of necessity spent a good deal of his time addressing letters backwards and forwards to himself, in one of his various capacities which would be read by himself at the next meeting, and receiving the instructions for what was to be replied to himself, etc., etc.

To overcome the problems of clerking and attending the numerous committee meetings he devised the simple but ingenious expedient of arranging for all committees to be composed of the entire council which could thus at any time in the course of its normal meeting resolve to go into committee of 'whatever' whereupon the public and press would retire from the chamber, the Chairman of the Council would exchange seats with the Chairman of the Committee, and proceedings so continue.

Lest any reader should feel that Lewis already held more than sufficient public appointments for one man to handle, he would indeed be mistaken for the foregoing represents but a small part of his multifarious public offices which all carried their appropriate emoluments. The next most important was the Clerkship of the Billericay Board of Guardians which administered the Poor Law for 26 parishes stretching from South Weald to Bowers Gifford, and managed the Workhouse at Billericay. He could also find the time to perform the duties of Clerk to the Justices at Brentwood Police Court, and similarly for the Billericay Magistrates. In between the above commitments he fulfilled the position of Superintendent Registrar of Births, Deaths and Marriages for the Brentwood and Billericay sub-districts.

Outside the sphere of public appointments C.C. Lewis was Chairman of the Brentwood Town Hall Company in which building the Council rented one room for its office, but only hired a room as its council chamber as required. He was also a director of the local gas company and served on the local hospital management committee. It will therefore come as no surprise to readers to learn that it was generally held that no public meeting of any importance could be arranged until Mr. Lewis had consulted his diary. No doubt these arrangements will have saved the ratepayers a good deal of money, and as a corollary it will have been an equally lucrative arrangement for its incumbent.

In the early 1930's the whole pattern of local government changed as a result of a Government Review Order out of which the enlarged Urban District was formed, and Billericay elevated to the status of an Urban District Council. The work of the Board of Guardians of the Poor also terminated about this time when it was transferred to the Public Assistance Committee of the Essex County Council and the workhouse now became St. Andrew's Hospital.

It is hoped this collection of pictures comprised in the two little books taken together will provide readers with a fairly comprehensive view of how the town and district appeared during the period covered. Cross reference between the plates in this book and those in the first volume are distinguished by placing a figure 1 with an oblique before the relative plate number, thus 1/... for a plate in volume one.

I take this opportunity to offer thanks to all those people who helped me to build my collection of Brentwood pictures, postcards and ephemera, and to hope that readers will find this volume to be no less enjoyable than its predecessor.

Llanvair Kilgeddin, Gwent   Frank D. Simpson

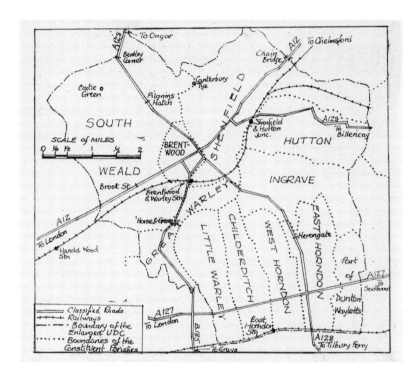

1. A sketch plan to show the limits of the enlarged Brentwood Urban District, together with the boundaries of the former separate parishes. It will be readily seen how small was the area administered by the first urban authority.

Eastern Counties Railway.

2. A historic picture of one of the first railway trains (Eastern Counties Railway) to come to Brentwood in 1842 copied from a contemporary painting in the author's possession, said to be painted by a member of the Palmer family which had a flourishing business shoeing the horses for the coaches and other road traffic much of which was lost to the railway. On the train is the Bury coach which completed its journey that way until it was found it was easier for its passengers and baggage to be placed directly on the train.

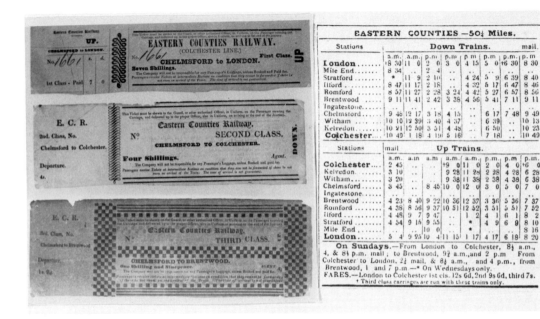

3. If you had come to Brentwood by the train in the previous plate you would have been given a ticket like those shown above, these were torn from a book, hence the term 'Booking Office', and you would have chosen your train from the timetable above in force from the opening to Colchester. Note that there were then only eleven stations on the whole line; each had its own colour of ticket which had one, two or three black lines at top and bottom to indicate your class of coach for easy checking, but soon rendered obsolete when the number of stations exceeded the colours available.

The Parade, "showing Cinema" Brentwood.

127.

4. A now vanished scene taken from the former station bridge in the 1920's showing that old favourite place of entertainment, the Parade Cinema which closed its doors about 1940: it was used later by a firm of motor factors bombed out of Southend-on-Sea. To the left is Barrett's Coal Office, later Hudson's, next is Smith's Domestic Store which continued by a van round when the shop became Herbert's Fish and Chip Saloon. Nothing now remains of any of these buildings, all is demolished and re-developed.

The Annexe, Brentwood School.   No. 1520

5. Ingrave Road about 1929 showing the new dormitories and changing rooms which linked the 'Old Big School' to the headmaster's house: compare with plate 1/7: note also the newly planted pair of replacement 'Sister Elms'.

Wilson's Corner, High Street, Brentwood.

6. An early 1930's view of Wilson's Corner for comparing with plate 1/12. Here we have the newly erected high level gas lamps which were extinguished forever in 1939 for the 'black-out' and replaced post-war by electric lamps: note also the high but short lived lamp in the centre of the cross roads which caused more traffic problems than it solved. Notice also that Belisha Beacons have arrived, but the double telegraph poles have not yet been removed.

7. A 1933 view looking into St. Thomas Road from High Street showing the former garage of Rippon Bros., of which only the front two storey portion remains as part of The Arcade. Compare with the view taken from the other way in plate 1/16: the bus is one from the City fleet obtained from Westcliff Motor Services when the City took over its London-Southend route.

Brentwood, High Street.

A. F. S.
BTW 10.

8. A 1930's postcard view of the north side of High Street showing the properties that were erected on the site of the Manor House which can be seen in plate 1/20. The modernised 'Palace Cinema' may also be clearly seen.

9. This is a reproduction of a painting depicting Nos. 36 and 38 High Street, and the once famous Chequers Hotel showing its old plastered front; right is the old chapel. Many will remember the shop at the left as Cramphorn's Corn and Seed Store: the house next was Cullens grocery for many years before becoming Mence Smith's hardware store. Unfortunately the picture is undated, but is considered about 1845-1850.

The Thomas Becket Chapel, Brentwood.   No. 1736

10. A postcard taken from the north-west corner of the former Odeon Cinema. To the left is the end of the Lion and Lamb Hotel, next are two very old properties 59 and 61 High Street, a butchers and confectioners shop, and right is MacFisheries new premises, a name now no longer with us which replaced the old fish shop of Mr. French and Bardwell's china and glass shop.

11. An early postcard of the Lion and Lamb Hotel as it was about ninety years ago, of a very uninspired design the hideous notices do nothing to improve its appearance.

The High Street, Brentwood.

12. A late 1920's postcard of the last subject now considerably improved in appearance after refronting and general modernisation. The sign of The Chequers is visible on the right and the tall gabled building in the centre is Sainsbury's new provision store: see also plate 1/19, also newly erected.

13. Readers will find this location difficult of identification: it shows a former nursery ground located to the rear of Barclays Bank and the adjoining shops, viewed looking towards the villas in North Road Avenue: the two houses facing the camera are in Chestnut Grove: much of this land was built over with the new Territorial Army Drill Hall.

DAREN BREAD

REFRESHMENT REFRESHMENT
ROOMS ROOMS

LARGE ROOM
FOR PARTIES
CYCLES STORED FREE

DINNERS TEAS
& LUNCHEONS
AT POPULAR PRICES

WILDISH & SON Confectioners

CADBURY'S CHOCOLATE

WEDDING & BIRTHDAY
CAKES
MADE TO ORDER
CAKE & BUNS
SCHOOL TREATS

ENTRANCE FOR
CYCLES
THRO THE ARCH

TEA ROOMS   UP STAIRS

WILDISH & SON, Grocers, Bakers,
Confectioners & Caterers,
58 & 79, High Street, BRENTWOOD.
Dinners, Teas, & Light Refreshments. Large or small
Parties catered for.   Established 1880.

14. 58 High Street as it appeared in an advertisement dated 1908 when it was Wildish's bakery and pastry-cooks: they also traded from 77 and 79 on the other side of the street as grocery and domestic stores. By 1920 the shop was in the hands of D.W. Cullen before passing to Norrish's who transferred the business to a new restaurant a few doors lower down. It was then occupied by the Sun Stores, a cut price packet grocery. Notice the extensive use of china letters affixed to the glass windows, a now vanished form of advertising.

15. These premises lay next to those in the last plate, which comprises a chemists (H.A. Clarke) previously Hodgson & Son: next is Harridges, newsagent and tobacconist for many years: between comes the narrow entry into South Street, originally Chapmans Alley. Right are 64 and 66 as occupied by Boon, baker, and Lewis's, butchers, and then Norrish's new premises, later acquired by Hodges.

16. An excellent pen and ink sketch showing the rear of 60 and 62 High Street as seen from South Street: unfortunately neither artist nor date are known, but probably about 1900. There has been much redevelopment of late in the South Street area.

17. Middle High Street looking west about 85 years ago, which continues on from plate 13 when nos. 68 and 70 were in the occupation of George Yull whose family were plumbers for over a century, and George Aldridge who was the last saddler and harness marker in the town, who latterly turned to dealing in cycles.

18. The rear of the former George and Dragon Inn from a lithograph by Bamford of 1891. Notice the very narrow entry through to the High Street. The three storey property on the left was pulled down shortly after this was sketched to improve the very narrow entry into Crown Street; the next portion became the Dragon Boot Store of Dacombe, later Vidler the outfitter.

19. A postcard view in the yard of the White Hart Hotel which shows the old fashioned open galleries which had then been enclosed. Considerable further alterations and modernisation have since occurred.

E. P. Guest, Limited

Photographic and Store Chemists,

129 & 31, High Street,

BRENTWOOD.

MAIN ESTABLISHMENT, No. 129.

Can supply you with everything a Modern
Drug Store can produce at

London Store Prices For CASH.

PHOTOGRAPHY IN ALL ITS BRANCHES.

Developing and Printing   An Up-to-date Dark-room.
done in a Day.

ALL ORDERS ABOVE 5/- CARRIAGE PAID.

20. A 1908 illustrated advertisement of the large property comprising 129 High Street before it was divided about 1930, the centre portion remaining a chemist's under Mr. Hampton; the right hand section became Ellis's wireless shop, it was the first opened for this purpose, though for a short time it was in Kings Road. The far left was formerly the proprietor's house, next altered to Clarry's Valeteria and in 1940 taken over by H. J. Looker as an ironmongery shop.

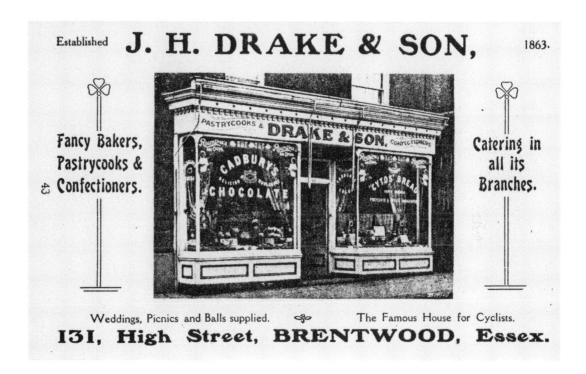

21. Another illustrated advertisement from the same source as the last when in occupation by the Drake's who carried on as bakers and pastrycooks for most of a century: the western boundary fronted onto North Street, now Western Gardens, see plate 1/36.

Brook Street Hill, Brentwood

22. This early view of Brook Street village was posted in 1907 to a lady in Oxford and shows the portion coming between plates 1/39 and 1/41. The premises on the right were occupied by Bennett's the undertakers for many years before moving up to lower High Street. The main road still bears a truly rural appearance even at this date.

384 The Alms Houses, South Weald

23. Returning from Brook Street via Vicarage Lane and South Weald after crossing the Bye-Pass Road one comes to these picturesque old Alms Houses with the tiny chapel which were built and endowed under the direction of Sir Anthony Browne in conjunction with the foundation of the Grammar School, now entitled Brentwood School.

24. Continuing in Vicarage Lane towards the church corner one comes to this beautiful scene well-captured in this postcard. One very interesting item captured by the photographer is the warning sign on the grass triangle formerly provided by the Automobile Association until standard Ministry of Transport signs replaced them.

South Weald, Rocketts Lodge

25. An early postcard view of the fine entrance to 'Rochetts', South Weald, in the early years of this century. The house was donated by a grateful nation to the Earl of St. Vincent for his services.

ST. PAULS, BENTLEY, SOUTH WEALD. 2063.

Fred Spalding & Sons
Photo
Chelmsford
Copyright

26. St. Paul's Church at Bentley from a postcard issued shortly after it had been built whilst the trees around were still relatively young: it was a daughter church to that at South Weald, to serve a district which was a considerable distance from South Weald, with its own parsonage house.

Navestock Church

27. Navestock is a large and scattered parish adjoining South Weald, containing over 4,000 acres. This card shows the church which contains a number of fine memorials to the Waldegrave family which at one time owned a very large portion of the parish.

The Swan, Doddinghurst.

28. A postcard view of the 'Swan' public house at Kelvedon Hatch close by the village pond complete with swans very appropriately, it was formerly in the ownership of Seabrook's Thurrock Brewery which was taken over by Charrington's in the late twenties. It is placed almost on the boundary with Doddinghurst parish just across the road.

The Eagle, Kelvedon Common.

29. This postcard shows Kelvedon Hatch's other public house, the 'Eagle' after some refurbishment by Mann Crossmans after taking it over from Fielders of the Brentwood Brewery, via The Old Hornchurch Brewery of Conron & Co.

Warescot Road, Brentwood   No. 453

30. Warescot Road looking towards its junction with Ongar Road photographed from its original termination where the old cinder path crossed the fields of flowers grown at Bishops Hall Farm to Hatch Road. Originally intended to link up with what is now King George's Road, a plan frustrated by the construction of the Bye-Pass Road, it remains a cul-de-sac. The tall chimney belongs to the Highwood Hospital.

31. Nearer the town, in Ongar Road, is a portion of the former Royal Laundry premises about 1923 when the second bay was under construction. Notice the old wooden scaffolding then used. In front is a Dodge van when newly delivered. The chassis was supplied by Guy's Quick Service Garage (later Henderson's followed by Scott), the body was built locally by Ellis & Son of King Edward Road, see plate 1/104: the lettering was by P. Littlewood whose work could be seen all over the town for many a year.

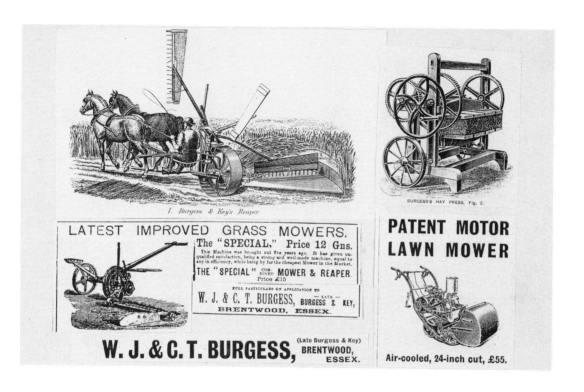

1. *Burgess & Key's Reaper.*

BURGESS'S HAY PRESS, Fig. 2.

LATEST IMPROVED GRASS MOWERS.
The "SPECIAL," Price 12 Gns.

This Machine was brought out five years ago. It has given unqualified satisfaction, being a strong and well-made machine, equal to any in efficiency, while being by far the cheapest Mower in the Market.

THE "SPECIAL" COMBINED MOWER & REAPER.
Price £15

FULL PARTICULARS ON APPLICATION TO

W. J. & C. T. BURGESS, BURGESS & KEY,
BRENTWOOD, ESSEX.

W. J. & C. T. BURGESS, (Late Burgess & Key) BRENTWOOD, ESSEX.

PATENT MOTOR LAWN MOWER

Air-cooled, 24-inch cut, £55.

32. Still nearer the town was the works of Burgess & Co which occupied the whole of the east side from Burland Road to the Castle Inn. See plates 34 and 1/51. This montage shows some of the products of that works. It closed circa 1922. Vast quantities of horseshoes were made here during the First World War for the military, waggon loads going away almost daily from the forges which one could see through the gate opposite the Victoria Arms Inn.

33. The administrative building of the former City Coach Co., which flourished until 1952 when it was nationalised and merged into the Westcliff Motor Services, in turn combined with 'Eastern National', which still uses the premises of its subsidiary Brentwood Engineering Coy reached from North Road, the above building being acquired by British Thermos Ltd. The City Coaches enjoyed an immense goodwill, its brown and cream coaches will be remembered still by many with some nostalgia.

34. The Castle Inn in Ongar Road from a postcard viewed from the forecourt of the former Drill Hall. It was earlier known as 'The Cricketers', but no explanation has been evinced for the change of name. At the rear was a large barn used for storage by Mr. Taylor of the second-hand furniture shop at 34 Ongar Road: also for a garage for his motor van which was one of the first to be used in the town.

Brentwood, Westbury Road.

35. An early view of the junction of Westbury Road with Kings Road which has not much changed. However, considerable changes have been effected on either side immediately out of this view.

36. The 'UP' side Booking Office at Brentwood station which received a direct hit from an enemy bomb during the 'blitz' requiring its total demolition and reconstruction. The new shops stand on the site of the trees to be seen in plate 1/59: for a short time a Mr. Rendell had a small florist/garden shop here prior to moving to a site at the junction of Kings & Queens roads in the grounds of the Shrubbery.

GREAT EASTERN EXPRESS. G.E.R⁼ᵞ.

37. A fine coloured postcard by Raphael Tuck of 1910 of a Great Eastern Railway train hauled by one of the famous 'Claud Hamilton' locomotives. It is seen passing the former gasworks which ceased to be used after the local company was acquired by the Gas Light & Coke Coy of London. Beyond to the left was Brown's brickfields and kilns, famous for its special shapes of bricks, which closed about 1939.

38. Here is the little 'Simplex' petrol driven shunting engine which in 1922 released four heavy horses from their arduous duty of moving coal and other laden wagons into the private sidings at the maltings, the County Council yard and coal merchants depots: lines unsuitable for normal locomotives.

39. A postcard view showing the doubling of the railway whilst construction was in progress. Also to be seen is the once renowned 'Eastern Belle' All-Pullman Express which ran in pre-war summers to a different resort each day. The lower Cornsland development is not yet under way at the top of the bank on the right. The newly built large gas-holder in Wharf Road about this time can be seen above the engine shed.

40. Taken from an old coloured postcard depicting the Warley Hospital main building when it was still designated the Essex County Asylum. On plate 1/62 may be seen an aerial view of the whole establishment. The first portions of the scheme were completed for occupation in 1853.

The Horse & Groom Warley Road near Brentwood.

41. A postcard view of the 'Horse and Groom' public house taken soon after rebuilding early this century into a quite worthy building. Although always spoken of as being at Warley, it does in fact stand in South Weald parish. Notice the customary horse trough outside, and the delivery of beer proceeding on the right in Mascalls Lane.

VIEW FROM HEADLEY COMMON, GT. WARLEY

42. An undated postcard of Headley Common looking towards the town, in the distance left is the 'Horse and Groom' at the cross roads, Mascalls Lane left and Eagle Way to the right. The Marillac Home is situated in the wooded area on the right.

The Green, Gt. Warley,
near Brentwood.

43. A very nice early postcard view of the pleasant green at Great Warley looking towards
Tylers Common when it was just a quiet country lane, though still very pleasant today.
The 'Thatchers Arms' Inn is just off the picture to the right, and the narrow lane leading to
Boyles Court can just be seen. Happily, the buildings around the green still retain much of
their original character.

THE PARISH CHURCH   GREAT WARLEY.

44. The beautiful parish church at Great Warley built by Evelyn Heseltine of The Goldings (see plate 1/67) in memory of his brother, from a card produced soon after completion. It replaced an earlier church which had become unsafe, which was located very remotely in relation to the village almost on the boundary with North Ockendon.

45. The Waterworks Pumping station at Great Warley of the South Essex Water Coy: It delivered water from a reservoir up to the water tower near the Barracks which unfortunately collapsed when being filled for the first time. This provided the first piped supply of water to the district.

46. A view of Little Warley Hall from a postcard reproduction of an early coloured engraving in the Essex Record Office: it is one of the earliest examples of domestic architecture in the district.

The "Tips," Shenfield Common   No. 753

47. A 1920's postcard showing the scene over part of Shenfield Common taken from the top of 'The Tips', a great mound formed from the surplus spoil excavated from the railway cutting which has always been a favourite place for children to play. The school girl is wearing the contemporary uniform of the Girls High School whose new premises can be seen above the trees.

48. A closer view of the new Brentwood Girls County High School mentioned with plate 47 soon after completion. It replaced its earlier home at Montpelier House on the corner of Queens Road and Rose Valley, which had become too small. Some classes had been temporarily housed in the Grinsted Hall in Kings Road, or in the Billiard Room at 'Five Wells' the large house on the opposite corner, since demolished and the site redeveloped.

Shenfield Common.   No. 1066

49. This postcard view shows the upper part of Shenfield Common of about 1928 with the Artichoke Inn in the background: the long low building to the right is the former brew-house, the white strip thereon covers the name board of the former Brentwood Quoit Club which had its ground here, now a bowling green. The writer can recall the clink of the quoits as a small boy when passing. Is the game of quoits played any more?

Thorndon

50. The first Thorndon Hall reproduced from an old print, it stood about half a mile distant from the site of the present Thorndon Hall which was gutted in a disastrous fire in 1878. The Petre family has since lived at Writtle Park or at Ingatestone Hall. See also plate 1/84.

Brentwood Ingrave Church

51. This 1908 postcard shows the present Ingrave Church which was erected in 1738 by Robert Lord Petre when the parishes of Ingrave and West Horndon were united ecclesiastically, and both of the former churches were pulled down. Lord Petre was also patron of the livings at Ingatestone with Buttsbury: of Mountnessing and of Childerditch but being a Roman Catholic cannot present. The interior is of unusual design being planned rather on the lines of a collegiate chapel.

THE RECTORY, INGRAVE 1993.

Fred Spalding
Photo
Chelmsford
Copyright.

52. The new rectory at Ingrave as seen in a postcard issued about the time of its opening about a hundred years ago; it is quite a large building of pleasing appearance which replaced an earlier residence described as a 'plain but comfortable old English'.

53. The footpath from Priests Lane to Hanging Hill Lane which crosses the railway by Thrift Wood over a high footbridge, used to cross the track on the level approached by a steep path as can be seen in this view, a fine vantage point for train watching. The buffer stop to be seen on the right was the end of a long refuge siding which disappeared with the old Ingrave signal-box when the widening took place. The train heading towards London is hauled by an LNER formerly GER locomotive of the '1500' class, built about 1913.

SHENFIELD. 1642.

Fred Spalding. Photo. Chelmsford. Copyright

54. A view of the first houses to be built in Priests Lane about ninety years ago when the Glanthams Farm Estate was first being laid out for building purposes, still quite clearly a country lane.

SHENFIELD. 1638.

Fred Spalding.
Photo.
Chelmsford
Copyright.

55. The original Shenfield station as it appeared from under the arch from Hutton, consisting of booking hall and station masters house about 1908. Compare with plates 1/96 and 1/97. There are no other buildings in sight.

56. A view of the interior of the reconstructed station after widening of the line (see plate 1/95) but looking well-suited for its purpose: its appearance will now have changed somewhat with all the overline electrical catenary.

57. The foot of Bishops Hill Hutton as it looked about eighty years ago before development in this area had started. Houses, shops and a service station now stand on the left, and other developments are now to be seen on the right. The former 'Junction Hotel', now simply 'The Hutton', has not changed greatly outwardly.

POPLAR TRAINING SCHOOL, SHENFIELD. 1646.

Fred Spalding.
Photo.
Chelmsford.
Copyright.

58. This is the former Poplar Training Schools, one of the many such institutions opened around the town. Until the London County Council took over, a familiar sight on Sunday afternoons was the march of the children in their blue uniforms behind the school band to Brentwood via the main road and returning via Priests Lane.

59. The newly developing shopping area and housing being built on the Collins Farm Estate on the main Billericay Road at Hutton as it was in the early 1930's.

Hine. 10.
Copyright

Brickley Estate, Hutton

60. A postcard view of Brickley Lane Hutton which has undergone considerable changes in recent years brought about by the new London County Council Estate, and the new industrial area near the Mountnessing railway siding.

SHENFIELD. 1647.

61. Hutton Road Shenfield from a card of about 1910 as seen from the opposite direction to plate 1/94, at which date it was often known as the Market Place, though no market was ever held here. The Glanthams Farm House stood on the right behind the wooden fencing, giving name to the estate development.

62. An early 18th century view of Fitzwalters House from an old engraving made when it was in the occupation of Thos. Wright Esq. who executed many improvements. The artist by including the 20th milestone from London (right) pinpoints his location; he has romanticised not a little by including the small boat on the infant River Wid which flows through the estate, and the inclusion of a coach and four in the drive.

Shenfield Corner.

63. The cross roads at Shenfield formed when Worrin Road was opened opposite to the Hall Lane which is scarcely recognisable today. The house on the left belonged to the village smithy just below, see plate 1/90. Worrin Road is so named after the former owner of the land.

64. A pre-World War I view of Shenfield Place which was the home of the Courage family for a great many years in its original state: in the 1920's it passed to the Bayman family which rebuilt it quite extensively, and laid out some of the land for house building.

Shenfield Road, Brentwood   No. 463

65. A view in Shenfield Road about 1930 at the point where the newly developing Mill Hill joins, formerly a part of the large Middleton Hall Estate.

Brentwood War Memorial.

143884.

66. The Brentwood War Memorial to the Fallen in the First World War as erected in 1921 which actually stands in Shenfield parish. It was originally intended that it should stand in the cross roads at the top of High Street, fortunately wiser counsels prevailed before it was too late. It has since been considerably altered to take into account those who lost their lives in the last war.

Newnham House, Brentwood School.   No. 1521

67. Newnham House, formerly Shenfield House, is one of the better buildings which have been saved from developers by their acquisition by Brentwood School for a boarding house. The dilapidated building to the right is the remains of a part of Wilson's Store that was destroyed in the great fire, but never rebuilt because of a dispute with the former owner of Shenfield House who claimed some rights over the land on which it stood. Happily the situation was resolved in the 1950's.

68. An historic photograph here: taken on the occasion of the final meeting of the Billericay Board of Guardians: the following members representing the Brentwood area have been identified: of those standing is No. 6 from left W.H. Connel (Shenfield): No. 10 is C.E. Lewis the Clerk and at 14 is D. Cornish (Hutton). Seated from the left 1 is Mrs. Partridge and 2 Mrs. Crawshay (South Weald), 3 W.E. Lane (Shenfield), 4 J.T. West (Brentwood), 5 H.E. Shilton (Shenfield), 6 and 7 are Mrs. Figgins and Mrs. Collis (Brentwood), and 19 A.W. Brenes (Hutton). See also a note in the introduction concerning the Guardians.

Mountnessing Church.

69. One of the less familiar churches around Brentwood is at Mountnessing with its wooden steeple and shaft which lies quite a distance from the village on a by-way which is little used. It possesses a number of memorial tablets to the Prescotts' and other families associated with Thoby Priory.

HILL'S
BRENTWOOD
BREWERY.

GOOD BEER IS LIQUID BREAD.

PALE

FAMILY ALES.

ALE

	Bar.	Kil.	Fir.
X	27s.	13s. 6d.	6s. 9d.
K	32s.	16s. 0d.	8s. 0d.
KK	40s.	20s. 0d.	10s. 0d.
XXXX	54s.	27s. 0d.	13s. 6d.
Pale Ale	54s.	27s. 0d.	13s. 6d.
Porter	36s.	18s. 0d.	9s. 0d.

70. An interesting advertisement for Hill's Brewery which stood off Myrtle Road, it may be seen in plate 1/77 before closing down. Notice that the most expensive ale could be obtained for only 2 1/4d per pint (pre-decimal coinage, about one new penny) and the cheapest was but half that amount. Date: late 1860's.

MIDDLE CLASS EDUCATION,

AT THE "SOUTH VILLAS,"
Opposite North Warley Church,

WARLEY ROAD.

CONDUCTED BY MR. AND MRS. REMFRY.

The course of instruction embraces all that is essential to a sound and thorough English Education, including Reading with Analysis, Plain and Ornamental Penmanship, Arithmetic, Mensuration, Book-keeping, Euclid, Algebra, Grammar and Composition, Geography, Mapping, History, Drawing, Stenography, &c.

Young Ladies, in addition to such of the above as may be deemed requisite, are fully instructed in every branch of Needlework. Hours of attendance, 9 to 12 a.m. and 2 to 4 p.m. Mrs. R.'s Pupils, 9.30 to 12.30 a.m. and 2.30 to 4.30 p.m.

Terms:—10s. 6d., 12s. 6d., and 15s. 6d. per Quarter. Preparatory Class 7s.6d. Latin, French, or Music, 5s.6d. per Qr. extra.

Religious Instruction imparted on broad unsectarian principles, and constant vigilance exercised over the moral habits of the Pupils.

BRENTWOOD
COMMERCIAL SCHOOL.

TERMS.

Board and Education, including French and Latin, Washing, Use of Books, Repairing Linen, &c.

Under Ten years of age ...... 25 Guineas per annum
Above Ten years of age ...... 27 Guineas   ,,
Italian, One Guinea per Quarter.

ADDRESS:

MR. HOOKE, BRENTWOOD

71. A pair of advertisements which cast some light on private education facilities in mid-Victorian days, when most was provided by governesses and private tutors. The scale of terms and the subjects contained in the curricullum make interesting reading. The first National Schools were built in Coptfold Road in 1869; these followed some earlier schools in various premises.

HIGH STREET, BRENTWOOD.

JOHN RUFFELL'S

SOAP,
CANDLE,
OIL,
COLOURS,
WHITE LEAD,
AND
VARNISH
WAREHOUSE.

Colours prepared for painting, in any shade. Pots & brushes let on hire. Paraffin and Colza Oils at agents' prices. Brooms and Brushes of every description, at maker's prices.

J. T. ELEMAN,

COOPER

AND

HARDWARE

DEALER

ONGAR ROAD, BRENTWOOD,

Supplies the following Articles :

Turnery Ware of every description, improved Cinder Sifters, Dairy Utensils, Box Butter Churns, improved Wood Taps, Brushes and Brooms of all kinds, and Brewing Utensils of every description.

☞ *Repairs executed in a substantial manner with despatch.*

𝔗urnery of every description

DONE IN THE BEST MANNER.

72. A pair of quaintly illustrated advertisements of trades that have now virtually vanished: almost all goods are now sold under the makers brand names, be it soap or paint, which was then ground and mixed by the vendor to the customers needs. Almost everything made by the cooper has been superseded by plastic ware, though for a time enamelled iron utensils held sway. The pictures would be provided by the local printer and were no doubt the best he could select from his stock blocks to cover most trades.

THE LARGEST, CHEAPEST, & BEST STOCK
OF
OVERCOATS, BUSINESS COATS
VESTS, AND TROUSERS,
Hats, Caps, Scarfs, Fancy Shirts, &c.
IS TO BE OBTAINED ONLY AT
C. D. TAYLOR'S,
BLUE HOUSE,
OPPOSITE THE POST OFFICE,
HIGH STREET, BRENTWOOD.

C. T. SUBMITS THE ABOVE PATTERNS OF
RIFLE CLOTHES & ACCOUTREMENTS,
*which he undertakes to supply Ten per cent.
cheaper than any other House.*

N.B.—Rifle Clothing supplied at the shortest notice.

73. An advertisement from the 1860's in which the illustrations appear today as something akin to fancy dress: these were supplied to the newly forming Rifle Volunteers of which the 1st Battalion (Essex Regt) was based in the town. The local 'F' Company was enrolled in 1859 using the old Drill Hall near the town end of Ongar Road. In 1905 it had a strength of 95 volunteers, but was soon after superceded by the Territorial Army as part of Lord Haldanes reforms.

SUCH,
THE CHEQUERS INN, BRENTWOOD.

Good accommodation for Man and Horse.

IND, COOPE, & CO.'S SPLENDID ALES.

RICHARD FROSTICK,
MECHANICAL CHIMNEY SWEEPER.

At the back of the King's Head, Back Street, Brentwood,

Begs to solicit your support, and trusts by strict attention to merit a share of your favors.

Work done for Builders on the lowest terms.

R.F. has got the best contrived Machines of all sizes for Sweeping Chimneys and Flues. Chimneys taken by contract if required. Clean cloths for upper apartments. Smoke Jacks cleaned.

I am known as the Brentwood Sweep,
My work I do both Clean and cheap;
And should your chimneys get on fire,
I will put them out at your desire!

RUMBALL,
COACH BUILDER,
Ongar Road,
BRENTWOOD.

Repairs on the shortest notice.

ROYAL MAIL,
ONGAR AND BRENTWOOD.

Leaves Ongar in the morning at 7.55 and in the afternoon at 3.45, meeting the Up Trains at 9.10 a.m. and 4.58 p.m.

Leaving Brentwood on the arrival of the Down Trains from London at 11.27 a.m. and 4.35 p.m.

74. A group of interesting announcements, especially that of Mr. Frostick in poetic vein who also indicates the lack of any firefighting arrangements at that date. Rumball's business was continued until about 1918 on the corner of Waterloo Road. The Ongar coach ceased in the 1880's when the mail was transferred to go by rail having been worked by Mr. West for about fifty years, after which a mail-gig ran to and from Kelvedon Hatch in charge of 'Ginger Deeds' who will be remembered still by older readers.

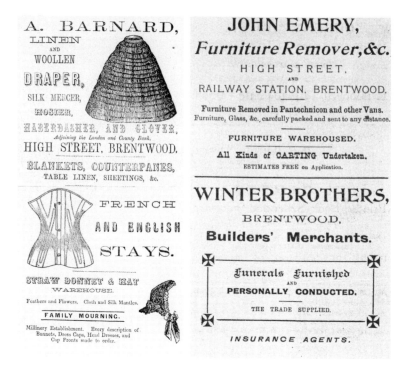

75. Left: Mr. Barnard occupied premises which in due course passed to the London Cooperative Society, the lower part of the advertisement is devoted to what was formerly a most important department of every such establishment, but now unknown. The illustrations here again have been drawn from the local printers stock blocks.

Right: A page from the Essex Almanac of 1905: John Emery also owned the steam mill in Queens Road of which no illustration has yet been discovered, it stood opposite the foot of the old Police Station Hill (now the library), it was powered by a beam engine. The Winters' business was continued for a short time by Davis of Romford until Churchill Johnson Ltd. took over, later moving to premises in High Street.

76. A photograph of a little 4 horse power Benz reputed to be the first horseless carriage to be owned in the town pictured outside the rather fine entrance to Middleton Hall to provide a suitable background for its obviously proud owner a local dental surgeon. It was first owned by a resident of Chelmsford; its registration plate was issued in December 1903 when that became a legal requirement, but the vehicle is of earlier vintage than indicated by the number, probably built in 1900 or 1901.